HOW *Government* WORKS

Declaring War

Fiona Young-Brown

Cavendish Square
New York

Published in 2019 by Cavendish Square Publishing, LLC
243 5th Avenue, Suite 136, New York, NY 10016

First Edition

Library of Congress Cataloging-in-Publication Data

Names: Young-Brown, Fiona, author.
Title: Declaring war / Fiona Young- Brown.
Description: New York : Cavendish Square, 2018. | Series: How government works | Includes bibliographical references and index.
Identifiers: LCCN 2018016567 (print) | LCCN 2018017116 (ebook) | ISBN 9781502640529 (ebook) | ISBN 9781502640512 (library bound) | ISBN 9781502640505 (pbk.)
Subjects: LCSH: War, Declaration of--Juvenile literature. | War (International law)--Juvenile literature.
Classification: LCC KZ6399 (ebook) | LCC KZ6399 .Y68 2018 (print) | DDC 341.6/2--dc23
LC record available at https://lccn.loc.gov/2018016567

Editorial Director: David McNamara
Editor: Caitlyn Miller
Copy Editor: Alex Tessman
Associate Art Director: Alan Sliwinski
Production Coordinator: Karol Szymczuk
Photo Research: J8 Media

The photographs in this book are used by permission and through the courtesy of: Cover National Archives/Wikimedia Commons/File:Franklin Roosevelt signing declaration of war against Japan.jpg/Public Domain; p. 4 Hulton Archive/Getty Images; p. 6 North Wind Picture Archives; p. 7 Ann Ronan Pictures/Print Collector/Getty Images; p. 10 John Moore/Getty Images; p. 11 Harold M. Lambert/Lambert/Getty Images; p. 12, 25 Everett Historical/Shutterstock.com; p. 14 Steven Clevenger/Corbis via Getty Images; p. 16 Brandon Bourdages/Shutterstock.com; p. 19 Ringo Chiu/AFP/Getty Images; p. 22 Alex Wong/Getty Images; p. 26 Library of Congress; p. 33 Sgt. Edward Zink/U.S. Army/Getty Images; p. 36 Fox Photos/Getty Images; p. 38 Mike Theiler/AFP/Getty Images; p. 41 AFP/Getty Images; p. 43 Dan Howell/Shutterstock.com; p. 44 Robert Nickelsberg/Getty Images; p. 46 CBS Photo Archive/Getty Images; p. 50 National Archives; p. 51 Hulton Archive/Getty Images; p. 55 Kent Nishimura/Getty Images.

Printed in the United States of America

CONTENTS

1 *What Is a Declaration of War?*

On December 8, 1941, the United States declared war against Japan. Just one day before, the naval base at Pearl Harbor in Hawaii had been devastated by a Japanese bombing attack. Within a few more days, the United States would also be at war with Germany and Italy. Over the next four years, more than sixteen million Americans fought in World War II in Europe, the Pacific, and North Africa. Nearly four hundred thousand US soldiers died, not including American civilian deaths. The total financial cost for the United States

Opposite: American soldiers land on the northern coast of France during the D-Day invasions, June 6, 1944.

George Washington speaks to the delegates gathered in Philadelphia for the Constitutional Convention in 1787.

alone totaled $341 billion (more than $4 trillion in today's money).

World War II is only one such example of the conflicts that the United States has been involved in since the nation's birth. The country itself was created after a war—the American Revolution, which ended in 1783. Therefore, war was at the forefront of the Founding Fathers' minds. When some of the Founding Fathers wrote the Constitution (the set of guidelines for governing this new nation), they thought carefully about the possibility of future wars. Who would have the power to declare such wars? Who would bear the responsibility? How can Americans make sure that war is not entered into without enough consideration?

Defining War

The United States fought with the Allies against Germany in World War I.

The word "war" usually brings to mind specific instances from past history, particularly World War I and World War II. War is openly declared by a government and is marked by the mobilization of the military to a front, the geographic area where the war is fought. Wars are official actions between nations. However, there are also civil wars, fought within a country. The Founding Fathers did not prepare for civil wars.

To complicate matters, most recent wars have not been officially declared as such. They are described using various terms: "conflict," "police action," or "military action." Sometimes they are labeled "humanitarian missions." A conflict is defined as an open, prolonged period of fighting. While it can be applied to one-on-one fighting between individuals, it is now, in many regards, interchangeable with war.

The terms used can play an important role in swaying public support. The public may support a series of "airstrikes" over a region while being opposed to a "war," which implies a long period of time with troops on the ground. Likewise, calling a military intervention a "counterterrorism operation" may sound more appealing

What the Constitution Says About War

Article 1 of the United States Constitution contains what is called the war powers clause. It explains the various duties of Congress within the government. Among those duties are tasks specifically related to war:

> *The Congress shall have power to ... provide for the common Defence and general Welfare of the United States.*
>
> *—Article 1, Section 2, Clause 1, US Constitution*

> *The Congress shall have power to ... declare war, grant Letters of Marque and Reprisal, and Make Rules concerning Captures on Land and Water; To raise and support Armies, but no Appropriation of Money to that Use shall be for a longer Term than two Years; To provide and maintain a Navy; To make Rules for the Government and Regulation of the land and naval Forces; To provide for calling forth the Militia to execute the Laws of the Union, suppress Insurrections and repel Invasions; To provide for organizing, arming, and disciplining, the Militia, and for governing such Part of them as may be employed in the*

Service of the United States, reserving to the States respectively, the Appointment of the Officers, and the Authority of training the Militia according to the discipline prescribed by Congress.

—Article 1, Section 8, Clauses 11–16, US Constitution

The Constitution quite clearly puts the declaring of war in the hands of Congress. When the document was being written, there was a lot of discussion as to whether the executive branch (i.e., the president) should be given sole power to declare war. However, several Founding Fathers, including Thomas Jefferson, believed it unthinkable that in a republic one man should have such power.

Parts of this constitutional clause are no longer considered relevant. The reference to "letters of marque" refers to an old practice of using privateers (an armed, private ship hired by the government) to attack enemy ships. This practice was outlawed in the 1856 Paris Declaration of Maritime Law, and the United States has observed this ban. But other parts are still relevant. With or without a declaration of war, Congress bears the responsibility for putting together an army and navy, as well as funding them and maintaining them. The president's war powers are defined elsewhere in the Constitution.

The US military helps with many humanitarian missions. Here, a soldier is delivering aid packages to hurricane victims.

than a war. That term indicates the operation is necessary to keep Americans safe from terrorists.

Technically, though, there is still a difference. A counterterrorism operation or a conflict is not identical to a war. The difference in which term is used determines the roles of both Congress and the president as laid out by the Constitution. In writing the document, the Founding Fathers took great care to ensure that power would be divided. They were escaping what they considered a tyrannical king. Therefore, they created several separate branches of government, each with different roles.

The decision to go to war is not one which is entered into lightly. Both Congress and the president should ideally work together to make such a decision and to then support the various branches of government until a resolution or peace is found.

War: Country and People

The parts played by the government and the Constitution are not the only important factors in declaring war. The decision to go to war is one that has enormous impacts on a country. There will be a mobilization of fighting forces. Will the mobilization be voluntary or will there be the reinstatement of a draft? Citizens who fight will put their lives on the line. Meanwhile, they leave behind families and communities who will also be affected. In the example of World War II, effects felt on the home front ranged from which foods were available in stores to massive changes in industry to support the war effort. Some effects would be the start of longer-term social

While soldiers are away fighting, people at home help support the war effort, just as these women did during World War II.

The American Civil War

The Constitution states clear rules for the declaring and waging of war against foreign nations. But what happens when the war is between citizens?

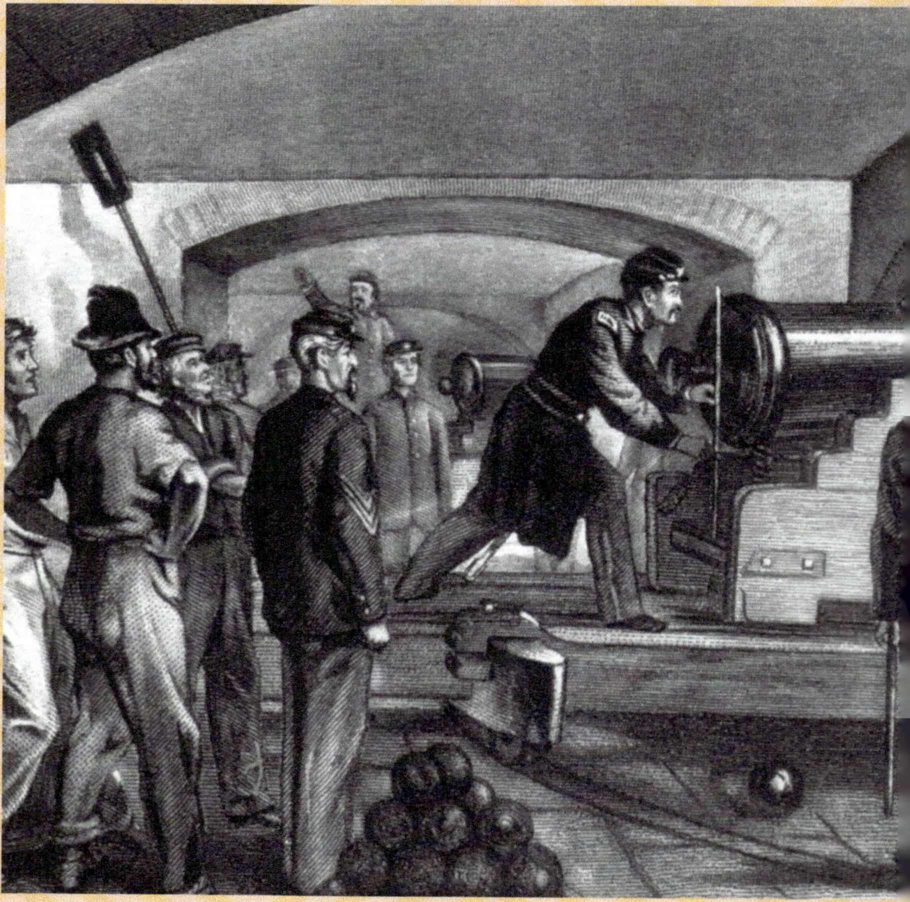

The Battle of Fort Sumter took place from April 12 to April 14, 1861. It was the first battle of the Civil War.

In December 1860, South Carolina formally announced its secession from the United States. Several other states followed suit. In February 1861, they joined to form the Confederate States of America (also known as the Confederacy). Jefferson Davis was sworn in as president of the Confederacy later that same month.

President Abraham Lincoln and Congress faced a problem. To declare war would be to recognize the Confederacy as a legitimate nation in its own right. For the same reason, Lincoln refused to negotiate with representatives from the South when they demanded Union troops to leave South Carolina's Fort Sumter. In April, Confederate forces began bombarding the fort with artillery. Those inside returned fire, but they were hugely outnumbered and gave up their position.

This was considered the first battle of the Civil War. Lincoln called for volunteers to put an end to the rebellion, but the South saw that as an act of aggression. Four more states seceded. Several days later, Lincoln ordered a blockade of all Southern ports. War was under way.

Despite the lack of an official declaration, several events could be considered declarations of war. These include secession by the South, the attack on Fort Sumter, and the port blockade by the North.

change. For instance, during World War II, women worked outside of the home in large numbers and gained greater freedoms. Other effects of war at home would be a source of ongoing shame decades later—the detention of Japanese Americans in internment camps, for example. Americans of Japanese descent were forced to leave their homes and live in detention camps for the duration of the war, in case they might try to help the Japanese enemy.

Wars can mobilize the public to rally either with support or to voice their opposition. After widespread support for World War II, the Vietnam War was met with fierce opposition that grew over time. There are many reasons for those differences in public support. Furthermore, public support—or lack thereof—has a major effect on the war itself.

Understanding War

The United States is a nation that was created by war. The American Revolution, from 1775 to 1783, resulted in many deaths. But it also resulted in freedom from the British crown and the birth of a new country. With the creation

Military actions have often faced opposition. Here, marchers protest the Vietnam War.

of a new country, people were free to create their own set of rules that would guide the nation through the coming decades and centuries.

When the Founding Fathers met to discuss these new rules, they wanted to avoid the type of government that they had recently escaped. They created the Constitution, the document that is at the heart of American government. As they wrote it, they paid careful attention to a number of topics. One of those topics was war. They wanted to make sure that if the nation needed to go to war in the future, the decision would not be made lightly. Nor would it be made by just one person. Therefore, they gave different responsibilities to Congress and to the president, expecting that they would work together.

The writers of the Constitution could not have imagined everything that would happen, but they hoped that they had provided the key guidelines. Over the centuries, as the United States has faced war against Mexico, Spain, Germany, and Japan, those words of the Constitution have been reread. Those in power have taken on the responsibility of following them in the manner they think best.

2 *Who Declares War?*

The Constitution of the United States divides the federal government into three ruling bodies. The executive branch is the office of the president. The legislative branch is both houses of Congress. The judicial branch is the Supreme Court. The roles and duties of each branch are laid out in the Constitution.

As previously mentioned, Article 1, Section 8 of the Constitution contains what is known as the war powers clause. It states that the legislative branch of government is responsible for making declarations of

Opposite: Throughout the years, Congress, housed in the Capitol Building, has debated when and if the United States should go to war.

war, and for funding and maintaining military forces. To fully understand the war powers clause and how war is declared, we must first take a closer look at each of the branches of government.

The Legislative Branch

The legislative branch, or Congress, consists of two separate chambers. The House of Representatives is the so-called lower chamber of the two. This is common in many governments around the world. The "lower house" has more members and is sometimes thought to have more power, while the upper house (in this case, the Senate) is smaller. There are 435 voting members in the House, one per voting district of each state. The voting districts are based on population size. This means that states with a larger population will have more representatives. For example, California has more than fifty representatives, while states such as Alaska and Montana each have just one. There are also six nonvoting members. These nonvoting members represent the District of Columbia and five overseas US territories. Representatives are elected in their districts and serve a term of two years. The Senate, or upper chamber, has far fewer members than the House. Each state has two senators, and they serve a term of six years. There are no limits on the number of terms either can be reelected.

Voters complete their ballot forms in a presidential election. The president is then officially chosen by members of the electoral college.

The Executive Branch

Although the Constitution grants Congress the power to declare war, it is the president's job to decide how the war should be fought. The president is not elected directly by the people. Instead, the electoral college elects the president after a popular vote is tallied. Each state appoints a number of electors to match their number of representatives and senators. Each state also sets its own rules regarding how the electors vote. In some states, the winner of the popular vote gains all of the electoral college votes. In other states, the number of electoral votes may be decided proportionally. This means that it is possible for a candidate to win the popular vote but for their opponent to win the electoral college vote. Whoever wins the electoral college vote becomes president. Once elected, the president serves a term of four years. Since the enactment of the Twenty-Second Amendment in 1947, a person can serve no more than two terms as president.

Article 2, Section 2 of the Constitution begins: "The President shall be Commander in Chief of the Army and Navy of the United States." This clause gives the president the power to instruct the military, but his power as commander in chief has limits. One of those limits is that Congress, rather than the president, declares war. In other words, the two clauses are intended so that both branches, executive and legislative, work together in times of war. Neither branch has sole power.

The separation of powers was a deliberate move by the framers of the Constitution so that no one person would hold absolute power. Founding Father Alexander Hamilton said:

> *The President is to be commander-in-chief of the army and navy of the United States. In this respect, his authority would be nominally the same with that of the king of Great Britain, but in substance much inferior to it. It would amount to nothing more than the supreme command and direction of the military and naval forces; while that of the British king extends to the declaring of war and to the raising and regulating of fleets and armies—all which, by the Constitution under consideration, would appertain to the legislature.*

Hamilton was comparing the power of the president to that of the British king, and he was noting some important differences. The king commanded the army and navy, but he also had the power to declare war. In the Constitution, while the president commands the army and navy, Congress declares war and has the responsibility to maintain the military. Hamilton wanted to show that the president did not have the same powers as a king.

Founding Father James Madison served as president from 1809 to 1817. He explained that the acts of declaring war and waging war must be kept separate. This was to make sure that war was never declared "for the sake of being conducted." Madison thought that the war powers clause was one of the most important parts of the Constitution because "the executive is the branch of power most interested in war." He worried that the president might be too eager to go to war. He hoped that Congress would be more thoughtful and avoid making a hasty decision.

As the commander in chief, the president can decide where troops should be stationed. The president gives orders to the generals and admirals who lead the various military branches. But the president's other powers have been debated by many historians and scholars. Some believe that as commander in chief, the president can do what he chooses with the military and when, with or without the approval of Congress. Others disagree. They say it gives him oversight of the military, as a civilian outsider.

The nine-member Supreme Court, the judicial branch of the US government, rarely involves itself in matters of war.

The Judicial Branch

The judiciary plays a pivotal role in matters of war. The nine members of the Supreme Court were all nominated by a president. The Senate then voted on whether to confirm the nominee. Once appointed, a Supreme Court justice may hold the seat for life, or until he or she chooses to retire. Then the nomination and confirmation process for that seat begins again.

For the most part, the Supreme Court has chosen to not become involved in affairs of war. Only a few cases related to war have ever gone before the court. Based on those outcomes, the justices are unwilling to take any big steps in limiting the actions of either the legislative or executive branch. Many historians would argue that such intervention was rarely needed in the early decades of America's history. Congress took the initiative when it came to foreign policy. The legislators were quick to step in if it appeared that a president might be trying to overstep his bounds during peacetime. In this manner, they were able to avoid situations that might lead to war.

The Rise of Emergency Powers

One of the most notable occasions when the Supreme Court did attempt to rein in the president was at the outbreak of the Civil War. In 1861, President Lincoln decided to suspend habeas corpus. This is a part of the law that rules you must bring a prisoner to court so that a judge can hear what the person is being charged with and if they have been charged properly. It makes sure that due process has been followed. However, Lincoln said it was necessary to ignore the law in order to put an end to the growing rebellion in the South. The Supreme Court said that he could not do this. In a bold move, he simply ignored the Supreme Court ruling. The prisoner in question, a politician from Maryland, continued to be held without trial in a military prison. Five years later, the Supreme Court would rule on a similar case. They said that only Congress had the power to end the rule of habeas corpus. They also ruled that civilians could not be held or tried by military courts, even during times of war.

The ruling was important. Perhaps even more important was the precedent that Lincoln set by choosing to ignore it. It paved the way for future presidents to claim special executive powers during times of war. The Constitution does not grant any particular powers in

President Roosevelt's Infamy Speech

The last official declarations of war from Congress were made during World War II. President Franklin D. Roosevelt, as commander in chief, officially made the first request of the World War II era to Congress on December 8, 1941. Just one day earlier, Japanese forces had bombed the US naval base at Pearl Harbor, killing 2,403 Americans.

President Roosevelt's speech was quite short compared to many famous political speeches. He spoke for about seven minutes to a joint session of Congress. The speech was also broadcast to radio audiences across the country.

He described the day of the attacks as "a date which will live in infamy." He went on to explain how the attacks had clearly taken some weeks to plan. At the time of the actual bombing, the government was still discussing with representatives in Japan how to maintain peace in the Pacific region. Therefore, he reasoned, "the Japanese Government has deliberately sought to deceive the United States by false statements and expressions of hope for continued peace." The president referenced his own constitutionally approved position as commander in chief. He stated that he was requesting all necessary measures for the protection of the country. He concluded his speech: "I ask that the Congress declare that since the unprovoked and dastardly attack by Japan on Sunday, December 7, 1941, a state of war has existed between the United States and the Japanese Empire."

Within an hour, Congress had voted upon and approved a declaration of war. The speech is now considered one of the most famous from the twentieth century. Congress would declare war with six more nations during World War II.

The United States entered World War II after the Japanese bombings of Pearl Harbor in December 1941.

During World War II, Japanese Americans were rounded up and sent to live in internment camps such as this one in California.

a national emergency, but presidents have increasingly claimed such powers.

President Woodrow Wilson believed that the president should be completely in charge of the nation. He should guide Congress rather than allowing them to tell him what to do. In 1916, he asked Congress for legislation to censor the press, or decide what journalists could and couldn't say. When his censorship plan failed, Wilson established the Committee on Public Information to influence public opinion via the media.

By the time World War II was on the horizon, all three branches of government seemed to have accepted the existence of emergency war powers that were held by the president. After all, Lincoln and Wilson had adopted them. This too was a time of national emergency. Congress was more than happy to give the president hugely expanded powers. They said it was for the sake of the war effort. Under President Franklin D. Roosevelt's direction, many new agencies were created, including the Office of War Information, the Office of Civilian Defense, the War Production Board, and the National Defense Research Committee. Roosevelt allowed for all sorts of resources and businesses to be diverted to the war effort, with no opposition from the Supreme Court. What's more, the Supreme Court ruled that the president was completely within his rights to apply sanctions (economic punishments) to any unions or industries that failed to comply with new wartime rules. Most notably, the Supreme Court upheld that Roosevelt had the right to create Japanese internment camps. In the case *Korematsu vs. United States* (1944), the justices agreed that Congress had approved the relocation of Japanese Americans as a joint action. After all, they had ratified Roosevelt's executive order. Detaining American citizens was considered a matter of national security.

The Korean War: Changing Roles

Article 1, Section 8 of the Constitution states that Congress has the power to declare war. However, it does not provide any sort of guidelines as to how they should declare war. Nor does it say what form any declaration must take. This means that there has been a move away from presidents requesting formal approval. Instead, if Congress approves the funds for the military, this is viewed as a de facto agreement to wage war. The lines between declaring war and waging war have become increasingly blurred. We can see that over time the office of the president has claimed more powers as commander in chief. As such, many in the office have stated that they alone have the authority to act. They say it does not matter if Congress gives permission. This would seem to be in direct contrast to what the framers of the Constitution originally intended.

The last formally declared war was World War II. Since then, the American military has fought in a number of wars, but these have all been committed to without an official declaration. Most have been the result of the commander in chief exercising their claimed right to command the military.

Adding to the problem of who should declare war and how is the fact that the world has changed greatly since the end of World War II. President Roosevelt created dozens of new agencies during that war. After hostilities ended in 1945, the Cold War with the Soviet Union became a new priority. The Cold War was not a military action. It was an ongoing period of open tension between the United States and the Soviet Union. Both were constantly trying to prove their superiority. In 1947, President Truman took some of the offices created by Roosevelt and turned them into permanent positions. The joint chiefs of staff, the secretary of defense, the National Security Council, and the Central Intelligence Agency (CIA) all report directly to the president rather than to Congress. Executive power increased greatly, while legislative power weakened. This was demonstrated in 1950.

In 1950, North Korea launched an invasion of its southern neighbor and was easily able to take over much of the country in a relatively short time. Truman believed that the United States should go to war against North Korea to prevent the spread of communism and as a show of strength. There was a problem, though. He did not think that Congress would approve of any action. After all, the nation was still recovering from war and the hostilities in Korea did not place the United States in direct danger. They had not been attacked.

Truman put pressure on the United Nations to take action. Once they agreed, he argued that the United States was treaty-bound to take part. It was not a war but a "police action." When questioned about his authority, Truman claimed both Congress and the Supreme Court had "repeatedly recognized" the president's ability to go to war without authorization from any other branch of government. Of course, he could not produce any such evidence, but he insisted it was so. And so it has been ever since. His insistence that approval was not needed set the precedent for future presidents.

The Supreme Court did step in to restrain Roosevelt's successor. The Korean War was the first war not to have been declared by Congress. Instead, President Truman insisted that the military was participating in an international police action. Congress's permission, he reasoned, was not needed. However, it was not this detail that would be argued before the Supreme Court but another regarding limits of the president's power.

During the Korean War, a nationwide steelworkers strike seemed likely. President Truman said that if the steel mills shut down, military production would grind to a halt. This would cripple the war effort. Therefore, he used his power as commander in chief to order that the secretary of commerce seize all of the mills and operate them on behalf of the government. A case, now commonly known as the Steel Seizure Case, was heard by the court in 1952. They ruled that the president was not acting constitutionally when he attempted to seize the steel industry. As soon as the Supreme Court produced their ruling, Truman ordered that the mills be returned to their owners. The steelworkers went on strike, as predicted. The strike continued for nearly two months until the president threatened to find other ways to seize the mills, and the striking men returned to work.

To some historians, the decision was a strict scolding by the Supreme Court and an indication that the president's authority had limits, even at the time of war. Interestingly, though, the ruling said that it would probably be perfectly acceptable for the government to take over an industry, as long as Congress agreed. In the case of the steel mills, Congress had neither approved nor disapproved of the president's actions. Truman saw this lack of actual disapproval as a form of agreement. The Supreme Court argued otherwise.

The Vietnam War and the War Powers Resolution

By the 1960s, the issue of war had become much more controversial in the United States. As the decade progressed, opposition to the ongoing actions in Vietnam increased. Many attempts were made to challenge the constitutionality of the war in federal court. In particular, opponents of the war said that it was unconstitutional because Congress had never declared war. But the Supreme Court refused to hear any of the cases. They implied that war was a matter for the legislature to decide and not for the judiciary. Congress may not have approved a declaration of war, but they continued to appropriate funds, or set aside money, for military spending. This was seen as showing support for both Presidents Johnson and Nixon, two presidents who served as commander in chief during the Vietnam War.

It should be noted that although the Supreme Court refused to hear any of the cases, several justices did voice their opposition to the war. In the case of *Mora v. McNamara* (1968), a conscientious objector (someone who refuses to fight for moral reasons) said that since the Vietnam War was illegal, he was not breaking any law by refusing to fight in it. The Supreme Court said they would not hear the case. However, two justices did not agree with the decision. This suggests that a few may have believed that war had become a matter for the courts.

By 1973, the nation was suffering from heavy fatigue caused by opposition to the lengthy war in Vietnam. Members of Congress had grown angry with Presidents Kennedy, Johnson, and Nixon. All three had sent countless troops to Southeast Asia, many of whom would return injured or not at all. There had been no explicit

Congressional approval and no clearly defined goal. Instead, a generation of men had been fighting for reasons they didn't understand. To add to Congress's displeasure, it was discovered that Nixon had been secretly sending troops to fight in Cambodia.

As a result, Congress enacted the War Powers Resolution (WPR). The aim was to counter the actions of the president by placing limits on what he could do and for how long. The WPR stated that the president must inform Congress within forty-eight hours of committing any troops overseas. In addition, after sixty days, the president must seek an extension from Congress. Should he fail to do so, all troops must be withdrawn.

President Nixon was furious when he heard about the passing of the resolution. He described it as "a stab in the back" by Congress and quickly vetoed the legislation. Undeterred, Congress overrode his veto and the resolution was enacted.

The War Powers Resolution was not as effective as had been hoped. For one thing, presidents have simply ignored it, citing their position as commander in chief. Article 2, they claim, grants the power to order the military into war as they see fit.

In 1990, Iraqi troops invaded Kuwait. One week later, President George H. W. Bush informed Congress that he had sent a number of troops. He said that he had done so in accordance with the War Powers Resolution. More troops were sent, with a total of 350,000 deployed by the end of the year. A group of Democratic legislators sought a federal court injunction, or a ruling that would stop the president. They said that he should not take any further action without a Congressional declaration of war. However, the judge denied their request, ruling that there was not sufficient support for the injunction. By January 1991, the president had the support of the United Nations and so wrote to Congress. He asked for a resolution granting support, not permission. He stated that he did not need their permission since he had "constitutional authority" as commander in chief.

War in the Middle East and Authorizations for Use of Military Force

One way to avoid the official declaration of war while recognizing the powers of the president has been the Authorization for Use of Military Force (AUMF). This was first issued in September 2001, after the largest terrorist attacks ever to take place on American soil occurred on September 11 of that year. The AUMF gave President George W. Bush authority to use military force against those who had committed the September 11 attacks and "any associated forces." California Congresswoman Barbara Lee

US forces fight in Afghanistan in 2003. After the September 11 attacks, the president was granted an Authorization for Use of Military Force.

opposed the bill, concerned that it provided "a blank check for endless war." She has continued to oppose this and following AUMF renewals. By 2017, she had gained support from fellow members of the legislature on both sides of the political fence. Many were worried that the AUMF had been used to justify actions in multiple countries. This went far beyond the original intent in 2001. They proposed an amendment requiring the AUMF's expiration within 240 days. However, the amendment was removed by the rules committee. The AUMF is still in effect today.

So who really has the power to declare war? The answer is probably not as straightforward as you might think. If we base our answer on the Constitution as it was written, and on what historians tell us about the writings of the Founding Fathers, the answer seems clear. In order to avoid the United States repeating what they believed to be the tyranny of the monarchy (i.e., Great Britain), power should be split. Therefore, the entire government is split into three branches: the executive, the legislative, and the judiciary. The Founding Fathers behind the Constitution decided that declaring war should be carried out by Congress and then the war should be fought by the president.

That worked for more than a century. Over time, the world has changed. So has the way that war is fought, and so have the offices of government. Modern presidents have argued that being commander in chief is all the authority they need to order a military action.

When Congress Refuses to Approve a Resolution

In February 2015, President Barack Obama sent a proposed joint resolution to Congress. In it, he requested formal authorization to use military force against ISIS, a terrorist organization. For more than a year, members of the legislature had been repeatedly demanding such a proposal. However, when they received it, they refused to approve it.

Some have said that politics played a part, and that is most likely true. Some of the president's opponents said that the resolution would limit presidential powers too much, while others said it gave him too much power. At the same time, some of his supporters said the bill was too broad; others said it was too vague.

A similar occurrence had happened just two years earlier. President Obama had sent a formal request for approval to take military action in the Middle Eastern country of Syria, an ISIS stronghold.

In both events, Congress did not pass the resolutions, nor did they offer an alternative. Meanwhile, the military actions still went ahead, with Obama invoking his right to do so as commander in chief.

Some legal scholars have criticized Congress for their actions, saying that the president attempted to follow the demands of the Constitution. By failing to either approve or offer a solution, they proved themselves unwilling to take any responsibility for events in the Middle East.

CBS
MBS
CBS
NBC
CBS

3 *The Process of Declaring War*

According to the Constitution of the United States, Congress is responsible for declaring war. They also oversee the funds needed to fight that war. Meanwhile, the president is commander in chief. This makes the president responsible for the action of waging war, once Congress has authorized him to do so. No one person has exclusive power.

Furthermore, given that both chambers of Congress must agree in order to declare a war, it is assumed that there will be some discussion among the senators and

Opposite: President Franklin D. Roosevelt addresses Congress after the Pearl Harbor attacks to request a declaration of war.

Members of Congress gather at the Capitol to listen to a speech.

the representatives. During these discussions, members of the legislature will clearly define the reasons behind the decision to go to war. It also makes the aim of the war clearer. What is to be achieved?

Declaring War: Step by Step

Historically, the president has approached Congress to request a declaration of war. Both houses of Congress will then discuss the issue. For a declaration of war, they must issue a joint resolution. This means that both the Senate and the House of Representatives agree on the issue. In reality, by the time the president approaches Congress, it has typically been quite clear that war is imminent. In other words, there have been no occasions where the president has requested war when it is unlikely that Congress will agree. A joint resolution is voted upon and issued. It will usually declare that a state of war exists, and it will grant presidents authority to wage war as they see fit.

There have been no wars declared in this manner since World War II. Officially, the conflicts in Korea, Vietnam, Iraq, Afghanistan, and elsewhere have been just that—conflicts or military actions. As previously

Key War Votes in US History

The following dates mark the times Congress has voted on a resolution to declare war. (Both World War I and World War II involved more than one vote.)

1812 Congress approves war against Great Britain with a House vote of 79–49 on June 4 and a Senate vote on June 17 of 19–13.

1846 Congress approves war against Mexico with a House vote of 174–14 on May 11 and a Senate vote of 40–2 on May 12.

1898 The Senate and House unanimously approve war against Spain on April 25.

1917 Congress approves war against Germany with a Senate vote of 82–6 on April 4 and a House vote of 372–50 on April 6; Congress approves war against Austria-Hungary on December 7 with a House vote of 365–1 and a unanimous Senate vote.

1941 Congress approves war against Japan on December 8 with a House vote of 388–1 and a unanimous Senate vote; the House and Senate unanimously approve war against both Germany and Italy in separate votes on December 11.

1942 Congress approves three separate resolutions for declaring war against Bulgaria, Hungary, and Rumania. The House and Senate votes are unanimous.

mentioned, President Truman was reportedly afraid that Congress would not support a war in Korea. This is precisely why he didn't call it a war. Instead, he referred to it as a police action carried out by the United Nations. As a UN member, he argued, the United States was duty bound to assist. In latter examples, Congress has approved increased military spending and has given the president authority to act. But they have done this without a formal declaration of war.

Because there was no formal declaration, some experts and politicians have argued that the actions are unconstitutional. The Supreme Court has never been willing to hear such arguments, though. Even if Congress has not declared war, they have still given their approval for funding and military spending to support the war. Usually, this budget approval has been accepted as approval for the fighting.

No More War?

Why does the United States no longer declare war? It is not just the United States but most major world powers. Some experts say that there are legal reasons to avoid declaring war. Since World War II, a number of international laws have been put in place regarding how war should be fought. Ignoring these can lead to international trials for human rights violations and war crimes. If it is not a declared war but a military conflict, the legal guidelines are a little vaguer. For example, during the conflicts in Iraq and Afghanistan, private contractor companies have been used instead of soldiers for some tasks. Many of the prisons for detainees have been built and operated by private businesses. When the media has revealed the abuse of prisoners, certain legal issues can be avoided because it was not a military operation and therefore not subject to the same regulations. Furthermore, the government may not be responsible for the actions of a company.

Rather than seek permission to declare war, President Truman authorized a police action in Korea.

One potentially negative implication of not declaring war is that it may be difficult to understand the goals of the conflict. A declaration of war usually makes some reference to why the war is being fought and to what end. It may be to resist an invasion, to free a nation from a dictatorship, or perhaps to settle a trade dispute. Whatever the reason for the war, being clear about it makes it easier to define the purpose of the war. Is the goal to overthrow a government? To bring about democratic elections? When war is not declared in this fashion, the goals may be vaguer. This has been especially true in the series of conflicts in the Middle East all joined under the broad umbrella term the "war on terror."

In September 2001, shortly after the terrorist attacks that destroyed the World Trade Center in New York City, President Bush spoke to Congress. He announced the

Was Vietnam a War?

In 1950, President Harry S. Truman sent the first soldiers to Vietnam. They went as military advisors. By 1960, violence in the area was escalating, but the number of US troops there was still quite small. That changed in 1964.

On August 2, three North Vietnamese boats attacked a US naval vessel patrolling the Gulf of Tonkin. There were claims of a second attack on August 4 (but this was revealed to be untrue in 2005). Just a few days after the attack, Congress authorized and enacted the Gulf of Tonkin Resolution. The resolution allowed the president to take whatever military action he deemed necessary. At the time, many members of Congress insisted that this was not a declaration of war. Nevertheless, it gave the president virtually unrestricted powers.

Technically, the Vietnam War is considered a "military action authorized by Congress." In practice, regardless of the wording used, this was a lengthy and prolonged period of fighting, which is how many would define a war. It is an example of how the language used may have changed but the realities of combat remain the same.

The Gulf of Tonkin Resolution was repealed in 1970. By the time American troops withdrew in 1973, more than 58,000 had been killed, and more than 150,000 had been wounded.

The September 11 attacks marked the beginning of a lengthy military action in the Middle East

"war on terror." He said, "Our war on terror begins with al-Qaeda but it does not end there. It will not end until every terrorist group of global reach has been found, stopped, and defeated."

Some might say that the goal here is clear—to defeat terrorism. But that leads to questions of how do we define terrorism. Is it a realistic goal? If a clear enemy or goal is not stated, how do we know when it has been achieved? How do we know when the war is over?

Another reason given for the move away from declaring war is a practical one related to powers. Offices such as the secretary of defense, joint chiefs of staff, and the CIA all report to the president rather than to Congress. This has tipped the balance of power somewhat in favor of the executive branch. During both World Wars, the president was granted greatly increased powers. These included the right to detain foreign nationals on American soil and the right to take over businesses on behalf of the state for the war effort. There may be concerns that to declare war would set in motion these emergency powers. By not declaring war, Congress is helping to keep presidential powers in check.

Shifting Balances

As we look at the wars and military conflicts in America's history, and especially in the last eighty years or so, one fact is clear: the balance of power within the government is always shifting. While people may argue about the exact meaning of the Constitution and whether it is being followed, the reality is that military actions are

US Marines prepare to approach Baghdad in the 2003 invasion of Iraq.

still taking place. The method of announcing them may have changed. The way they are referred to has certainly changed. For example, in 2011 when Congress told President Obama that he must end the military action in Libya or request a proper extension, he replied that these were not "hostilities." They were "humanitarian aid" and therefore not a part of the War Powers Resolution. He later said, echoing many presidents before him, "As commander in chief I always preserve the right and the responsibility to act on behalf of America's national security. I don't believe that I was required to take this to Congress."

Yet whatever they are called, in the public eye they are considered wars.

4 *What Happens Next?*

President Lincoln once said, "In this age, in this country, public sentiment is everything. With it, nothing can fail; against it, nothing can succeed. Whoever molds public sentiment goes deeper than he who enacts statutes, or pronounces judicial decisions." He was talking about the importance of public opinion in the 1850s as the country edged closer and closer to civil war. Yet his words are just as accurate today. A war is not just fought overseas. It is also fought at home. Public support or opposition can have a huge impact on the outcome.

Opposite: Television coverage helped to change the public's view of war. Journalists such as Walter Cronkite, shown here during the Vietnam War, began reporting from locations where fighting was taking place.

During the Vietnam War, television made a huge impact in the way people saw war. Previously, the public had seen newsreel footage but only by going to the movie theater. By 1965, approximately 90 percent of American homes had a television. Nightly television news showed footage of the casualties and the damage done. Some say it is no coincidence that within a year, support for the war began to drop sharply.

When President Bush announced the "war on terror" in 2001, there was enormous political and public support for his actions. The nation was in shock after the September 11 attacks, which for many was the modern equivalent of the attacks on Pearl Harbor. People were mourning. They needed someone to blame. War, it seemed, would bring closure and revenge. It would punish those responsible.

More than fifteen years later, international support for the war has declined. In the United States, it has fluctuated continually, moving up or down depending on what is happening at any one time. In 2003, nearly two-thirds of Americans supported the military going to Iraq. By 2007, the same number considered it a mistake. One study showed that by the time President Obama announced that he was withdrawing troops from Iraq in 2011, 78 percent of the public supported him in doing so.

Public support is important for many reasons. It helps to maintain the morale of the troops serving overseas. It is also important to politicians. Their ability to be reelected depends on winning the approval of the voters.

The Peace Protests of the 1960s

One of the best-known and most active antiwar movements developed in response to the ongoing military conflict in Vietnam.

Opposition to the war began on a few college campuses. Opponents believed that President Johnson had escalated the crisis for the wrong reasons and without proper authorization from Congress. They were also aware of the fact that, due to the military draft, they would be called to fight. The peace movement started to grow after the United States began the heavy bombing of Vietnam in 1965. This sparked a number of marches and protests, although these were still mostly confined to college campuses and a few liberal groups. There was still strong public support for the war at this point.

That would change in 1968. Until then, most Americans thought that they were winning in Vietnam. The Tet Offensive, a series of coordinated attacks by North Vietnam, caused heavy casualties. People wondered why their sons and brothers were fighting so many miles away.

More began to resist the military draft. The peace movement was no longer limited to students. By 1968, only 35 percent approved of the way President Lyndon B. Johnson was handling the war, while 50 percent disapproved. American troops withdrew from Vietnam in 1973. Today, the war is often seen as proof that a long-term war cannot be won without public support.

Rosie the Riveter is a symbol of the women who mobilized on the home front during World War II.

Public support rises and falls for a variety of reasons, depending largely on whether the public feels as if their country is winning or losing a war. During World War II, the mobilization on the home front made people feel that they were part of the war effort. They also knew who the enemy was. Support was high. During Vietnam, the sight of so many injured soldiers returning home and the atrocities on the evening news, combined with only a vague sense of who the enemy was, contributed to the growing opposition. During the Gulf War, once again there was a clearly defined goal: to liberate Kuwait from Iraqi occupation. Once again, public support was strong. Many worry that as the "war on terror" drags on, the lack of a clearly defined enemy or a clear goal is lowering morale and weakening support.

Another factor that is having an impact on public support is the financial cost of war. The Constitution says that Congress is responsible for funding the military forces and for the other expenses of war. That money has to come from somewhere.

Funding a War

There are various ways to fund a war. The government has to find ways to either increase income (such as through

A 1942 promotion for war bonds

raising taxes) or to decrease spending in other areas (for example, cutting spending at home and diverting that money to the military). Otherwise, they face amassing huge national debt.

One common method of helping to raise funds for war used to be war bonds. These were used up to and including World War II. War bonds were made available to the public. The public would buy them or buy shares each week until they could afford a whole bond. They would be doing their part to help the war effort and it was treated as a sort of savings bond, although the rate of interest they would earn back was lower than a typical savings account. Buying them was seen as a patriotic duty. Everyone helped to share the debt of war. During World War II, eighty-five million Americans bought war bonds. Their total value was $185 billion toward funding the conflict.

Another way that money and resources were saved was through rationing. In the United States during World War II, gasoline and some foods were restricted. In the case of gasoline, rationing meant that this precious supply could be used for military and other essential purposes. Rationing was readily adopted, a sign of people's

The Military Draft

One question that is often asked is whether the military draft should be reinstated. Conscription is compulsory military service. It was widely used in the past. American men were subject to conscription in the Civil War, World War I, World War II, the Korean War, and the Vietnam War. Refusal to serve would result in facing trial as a conscientious objector. Punishments often included lengthy prison terms or even the death penalty.

From 1940 through 1973, a military draft was in place. This meant that, even during peacetime, men could be drafted into the military to fill necessary roles. Deferments could be granted to those in college, but this meant that during the Vietnam War, the fighting forces were disproportionately poor and nonwhite. A similar argument about the inequity of the military is heard today.

The draft ended in 1973 at the close of the Vietnam War. However, all US-born and some immigrant males between the ages of eighteen and twenty-five must still register for selective service. If for any reason the military draft is reinstated, a lottery system will be used to determine who is called upon first. Those aged twenty in the current calendar year would be called first, followed by those aged twenty-one, and so on up to twenty-five. Only then would younger men be drafted.

strong support for the war. Along with war bonds and tax increases, rationing helped the nation to take on the cost of war.

Funding for more recent conflicts has been very different. For one thing, people are less willing to pay increased taxes. In fact, they put pressure on politicians to cut taxes, meaning that Congress is forced to try and find funds elsewhere. Sometimes this means cutting spending at home. For instance, more money may be allocated to military spending while less is used for schools, roads, and other domestic needs. Yet this is still not enough to cover the massive costs involved in supporting troops overseas.

The answer is to borrow money and to increase the national debt. Since 2001, an estimated $2 trillion has been added to the national debt because of the "war on terror." Many of these funds have been borrowed from other nations, such as China. While people worry about the increased debt, the public and Congress are faced with the ongoing problem of how to fund a military conflict.

How Does It All End?

All too often, we imagine that a war ends as it does in so many movies. The enemy drops their weapons and surrenders unconditionally. The reality is usually very different. Many conflicts come to an end after lengthy negotiations of peace treaties. Even if there is a surrender, such as when Germany surrendered in World War II, treaties are then agreed upon to dictate terms of peace.

On April 30, 1945, Adolf Hitler committed suicide. Little did he know that some of his commanders had already been making secret plans to negotiate a surrender. Within a few days, those plans came into being, and on May 8, a document of unconditional surrender was signed by the German command. The date is commemorated as Victory in Europe (or VE) Day. Britain, the Soviet Union, and the United States had been meeting to discuss the terms of surrender for more than a year. In February 1945, President Roosevelt, British prime minister Winston Churchill, and Soviet leader Joseph Stalin all met in the Russian town of Yalta to finalize their terms. The surrender document covered a number of topics, including war trials of leaders, surrender of the troops and their return to Germany, and the exchange of prisoners.

Not all wars end so tidily. North and South Vietnam ended hostilities in 1975 and reunified the following year. However, the US military had withdrawn in 1973. Public opposition had grown to a significant level and there was little support for a war that had dragged on for so long. In January 1973, the signing of the Paris Peace Accords put an end to America's involvement in Vietnam. Negotiations had begun five years earlier but had ground to a halt many times as the different parties argued over territory and leadership. A few months after the accords were signed, fighting resumed between the north and the south. But by then, most of the American troops had left the area.

A soldier greets his family as he returns home from overseas deployment.

When some of the Founding Fathers gathered to write the Constitution, the United States was a very different nation to what it is now. They had to write a document that they thought would be applicable to them but which would remain relevant for centuries to come.

They chose to create a government where power was divided between different branches. The branches would need to work together, or one would keep another in check. This desire to split power can be seen in the war powers clause. Congress has certain powers to declare war and to maintain and fund a military. But once that war is declared, the president, the commander in chief, takes charge. Congress continues to oversee and approve.

Over time, the way those clauses are interpreted has changed somewhat. The most recent wars have not been declared by Congress. Instead, it is now accepted that when they approve funding, they are approving the military actions of the president. While some agree with this and others disagree, one fact remains. The government of the United States is a body of men and women continually working together to move forward, with the Constitution as their guiding rules. That is how government works.

Glossary

communism A political system based on the idea that all property is owned by the community and that everyone is paid equally.

conflict A serious disagreement or clash between two parties.

conscription Required enlistment for military service.

de facto (Latin) In fact; actually.

deferment Delaying or postponing an action. Usually used to describe the act of delaying military conscription.

draft A method of choosing men (and sometimes women) for required military service.

due process Fair treatment within the legal system according to the rules.

electoral college The group of people appointed to cast the formal votes for the president after the popular vote has been counted.

federal government The national government of the United States. It is made up of three branches: executive, judicial, and legislative.

front In military terms, the point where a military force is confronting the enemy.

habeas corpus A Latin phrase meaning "you have the body." It is now used in legal situations to mean that a person who has been arrested must be brought before a judge to show that they were arrested properly and for good reason.

home front The activities of the people in the country that is at war while the troops are fighting overseas.

joint resolution An agreement passed by both the Senate and the House of Representatives.

mobilization The act of preparing armed forces for military action.

national security Protecting the interests and safety of a country, both at home and overseas.

precedent An example or guide to be followed.

ratify Sign into law.

secession The act of formally withdrawing from a body or country. Most commonly used to describe the eleven states that left the Union, thereby bringing about the American Civil War.

war Armed military conflict usually between two countries, but sometimes between two regions or within a country.

Further Information

Books

Campagna, Daniel S. *We the People, Grades 5–8: Government in America.* Greensboro, NC: Mark Twain Media, 2002.

Demuth, Patricia Brennan. *What Is the Constitution?* New York: Penguin Workshop, 2018.

Websites

Bill of Rights Institute

https://www.billofrightsinstitute.org

On this site, find resources to learn more about the history and government of the United States.

National Constitution Center

https://www.constitutioncenter.org

The National Constitution Center was founded by Congress to spread information about and raise awareness of the Constitution. The site features a range of educational materials for students.

United States House of Representatives: History, Art and Archives

http://history.house.gov/Institution/Origins-Development/War-Powers

Part of the official site for the House of Representatives, this page presents the text of the war powers clause and explains the clause's history.

Videos

Franklin D. Roosevelt Addresses Congress, December 8, 1941

https://www.youtube.com/watch?v=5emI6lxlmjY

Watch President Franklin D. Roosevelt deliver his "Day of Infamy" speech to Congress in 1941.

Woodrow Wilson Asks Congress to Declare War

https://www.youtube.com/watch?v=rP_zPq7N4_c

Explore news footage of President Woodrow Wilson and the declaration of World War I in 1917.

Bibliography

Amadeo, Kimberly. "War on Terror Facts, Costs, and Timeline." *The Balance*, October 9, 2017. https://www.thebalance.com/war-on-terror-facts-costs-timeline-3306300.

Barron, David J. *Waging War: The Clash Between Presidents and Congress 1776 to ISIS*. New York: Simon and Schuster, 2016.

DeYoung, Karen. "Would Declaring 'War' on ISIS Make Victory More Certain - or Would It Not Matter?" *Washington Post*, July 17, 2016. https://www.washingtonpost.com/world/national-security/would-declaring-war-on-isis-make-victory-more-certain--or-would-it-even-matter/2016/07/16/ed95f0aa-4b6c-11e6-acbc-4d4870a079da_story.html.

Elsea, Jennifer K., and Matthew C. Weed. *Declarations of War and Authorizations for the Use of Military Force: Historical Background and Legal Implications*. Washington, DC: Congressional Research Service, 2014.

Epps, Garrett. "Yes, Congress Can Authorize War Without Formally 'Declaring' It." *Atlantic*, September 3, 2013. https://www.theatlantic.com/politics/archive/2013/09/yes-congress-can-authorize-war-without-formally-declaring-it/279261.

Franke-Ruta, Garance. "All the Previous Declarations of War." *Atlantic*, August 31, 2013. https://www.theatlantic.com/politics/archive/2013/08/all-the-previous-declarations-of-war/279246.

Jenkins, Brian Michael. "Fifteen Years on, Where Are We in the 'War on Terror'?" *The Rand Corporation Blog*, September 7, 2016. https://www.rand.org/blog/2016/09/fifteen-years-on-where-are-we-in-the-war-on-terror.html.

Kaine, Tim. "Congress Has a Role in U.S. Military Action in Iraq." *Washington Post*, June 24, 2014. https://www.washingtonpost.com/opinions/tim-kaine-congress-has-a-role-in-us-military-action-in-iraq/2014/06/24/77ec1776-fbc8-11e3-b1f4-8e77c632c07b_story.html?utm_term=.d89ebee81050.

Nichols, John. "Wars Should Be Declared by Congress, Not Merely Launched by Presidents." *Nation*, March 21, 2011. https://www.thenation.com/article/wars-should-be-declared-congress-not-merely-launched-presidents.

Index

About the Author

Fiona Young-Brown has written a number of books for young readers, including *History Makers: Eleanor Roosevelt: First Lady*, *News Literacy: Seeing Through Internet Hoaxes*, and *Great Discoveries in Science: Plate Tectonics*. She also enjoys writing about food, travel, and great apes. Originally from England, Young-Brown now lives in Kentucky with her husband and two dogs.